The Crocodile

Ruler of the River

text by Valérie Tracqui
photos by the BIOS Agency

 Charlesbridge

Library of Congress Cataloging-in-Publication Data
Tracqui, Valérie
    [le crocodile, terreur du fleuve. English]
    The crocodile: ruler of the river/ text by Valérie Tracqui;
photographs by the BIOS Agency.
        p.   cm.—(Animal close-ups)
    Includes bibliographical references (p. 28)
    Summary: Describes the physical characteristics, behavior, and
habitat of crocodiles, as well as efforts to protect these creatures.
    ISBN 1-57091-425-7 (softcover)
    1. Crocodiles—Juvenile literature. [1. Crocodiles.]
I. Title. II. Series.
QL666.C925T7313 1999   99-18761
597.98—dc21

Copyright © 1997 by Éditions Milan under the title *le crocodile: terreur du fleuve*
300 rue Léon-Joulin, 31101 Toulouse Cedex 100, France
French series editor, Valérie Tracqui

Copyright © 2000 by Charlesbridge Publishing
Translated by Lisa Laird

Published by Charlesbridge Publishing, 85 Main Street, Watertown, MA 02472
(617) 926-0329 • www.charlesbridge.com
Printed in Korea
10   9   8   7   6   5   4   3   2   1

The Nile crocodile lives in the lakes and rivers of Africa. It warms itself on the sunny shores, hides in the plants and trees at the water's edge, and builds nests for its eggs in the sandy banks.

Water and sunshine

During the rainy season in Africa, muddy rivers flood the plains and nearby lakes.

The Nile crocodile spends each morning lying in the sun. Around noon the reptile moves into the shade and opens its mouth wide to cool off. The crocodile slips back into the warm river water in the evening. It knows that water cools more slowly than air.

Like all reptiles, the temperature of the crocodile's blood changes with the air or water around it. The crocodile is almost always trying to warm up or cool down.

The crocodile's mouth is crisscrossed with blood vessels. On a hot day, it opens its mouth wide to let air blow over these veins, cooling the blood.

Scaly skin

The crocodile's skin is made up of individual scales. Each one falls off separately when the big reptile molts.

The crocodile can grow up to twenty feet long. On land it usually slithers slowly, but it can also walk with its belly off the ground and can even run up to ten miles an hour.

The crocodile has five webbed toes on its front feet and four on its back feet. Some species have powerful claws that they use to help them climb.

A fold of hard skin closes off the bottom of the crocodile's throat so that it can dive and eat without swallowing a lot of water.

You can tell a true crocodile from an alligator or a caiman because the fourth bottom tooth of a true crocodile sticks out when it closes its mouth.

Like the cat and the snake, the crocodile has a vertical pupil that gets smaller in bright light. At night the pupil opens wider so the reptile can see in the dark.

The crocodile has an incredibly strong jaw and rows of sharp teeth to help it catch its prey. But it does not use its teeth to chew food. They are actually quite fragile and often fall out. As soon as a tooth breaks, a new one replaces it.

The crocodile's nostrils are on top of its nose so that the big reptile can breath easily even when it is mostly submerged.

A muscular tail helps the crocodile lunge out of the water, surprising its prey.

The crocodile uses its webbed hind feet as paddles and its tail as a rudder when it swims slowly on the surface.

In the water

During the dry season the crocodile often spends long days underwater. Two valves automatically close over its nostrils and ears to keep the water out when it dives. It swims by moving its body from side to side and beating the water with its strong tail.

The crocodile may only come to the surface about once an hour to breathe. It will sometimes even swallow stones to make itself heavier and to help it stay balanced underwater.

The Nile crocodile has a very strong sense of smell and good hearing. Both senses help it to hunt and find a mate. It grunts, hisses, roars, and growls softly to communicate with others of its kind.

Transparent eyelids act like built-in goggles to protect the crocodile's eyes so that it can see clearly when it dives underwater.

Terror of the river

The crocodile has not eaten for several months. It looks just like a harmless tree trunk as it floats very slowly toward the bank. Hidden in the leaves along the shore, the crocodile stalks a group of zebras that have come to the river for a drink.

In the blink of an eye, the crocodile knocks a zebra down, hits it on the head with its tail, and drags it underwater to drown it. The more the zebra fights, the tighter the crocodile's powerful jaws squeeze.

An adult crocodile usually eats about once a week. If it had to, it could survive a whole year without eating.

Depending on its size, the crocodile eats insects, fish, birds, or mammals such as wildebeests, buffalo, or even monkeys when it can catch them.

The crocodile will sometimes swallow smaller prey whole, but it will have to eat the zebra in big bites.

Catching a snake is hard work! It slips, fights, and refuses to let itself be eaten. Crocodiles sometimes help each other hunt and then share the catch.

The Nile crocodile lives in a community group. Males and females stay apart except during mating season.

The Egyptian plover helps the crocodile by picking bits of meat from between its teeth.

A place for everyone

A big male claims a section of land and water. Other adults had better beware! When a female approaches, he swims on the surface to show how strong he is, forcing as much of his body out of the water as possible. The female quickly sinks her body almost totally underwater. She does not want to fight.

The female is looking for the best place to lay her eggs. She wants a sunny spot with soft earth that she can dig up easily. She will mate with the male that controls the territory she likes best.

Males and females spend several days together before mating underwater.

Hidden eggs

The female is ready to lay her eggs about five months after mating season. She is very aggressive now and fights with other females who come near her.

The mother-to-be digs her nest with her hind legs. When the nest is about two feet deep, she lays between twenty and ninety eggs inside and then covers them up with sand and dirt.

For three months she never lets the eggs out of her sight, and her mate stays close by. Too many predators would like to snack on a crocodile egg. When the big day arrives, both parents will open the nest and help the babies break out of their shells.

Beware of the monitor lizard! It can dig up crocodile eggs with its long snout and swallow them all in just a few seconds.

When her eggs are ready to hatch, the female crocodile rolls each egg between her tongue and the roof of her mouth to warm it and help break the shell.

The mother guards her nest carefully. She does not eat for ninety days and only rarely goes away to drink.

The watchful mother runs to her nest as soon as she hears the eggs begin to hatch.

Delicately she scoops up her newborns and carries them to the river in her mouth.

Baby crocodiles weigh less than one pound at birth.

The big day

The temperature in a crocodile nest is different in the middle than on the edges. Eggs that are either too hot or too cold will become females, while eggs that stay at a medium temperature will become males. All the eggs are white and only a little bigger than chicken eggs.

Tap! Tap! The first baby crocodile starts to break its shell. It lets out a small cry that its mother hears right away. She quickly uses her feet and nose to dig out the nest.

A baby crocodile breaks its shell with an egg tooth, a small horn that grows on its nose. The egg tooth falls off after birth.

A good mother

Baby crocodiles can swim as soon as they touch the water. They learn to swallow insects that pass close to their open mouths. But they have to be fast! Competition is fierce among them.

The crocodile mother constantly herds her babies together to keep them out of danger.

After their first trip to the river, the little crocodiles huddle up on solid ground. They will all live together in a nursery until they are about four months old. They take care of themselves, but the adult females in the community take turns guarding them and rush in to help if needed.

Baby crocodiles are only four to eight inches long when they are born, but they grow very quickly—almost a whole foot each year.

Hundreds of baby crocodiles live in a nursery. They stay warm by pressing against one another.

A marabou stork hunts on the bank of the river. It is looking for baby crocodiles hidden in the vegetation. They make easy prey.

Predator or prey?

Baby crocodiles have many enemies. Herons, spoonbills, and other aquatic birds hunt along the shore. Hyenas, jackals, and mongooses are all fast enough to catch and eat baby crocodiles. Even big fish like the silurid and river shark are enemies.

Living in a nursery helps the babies stay safe. A predator cannot eat all of them at the same time, and once warned, an adult will rush to defend them.

The young crocodiles learn to hunt and feed themselves. The biggest and strongest quickly begin to bully their smaller siblings.

When they leave the nursery, small groups of young crocodiles live in a burrow together until they are big enough to claim territory of their own.

Young crocodiles sometimes live far from the water. They are afraid of the bigger crocodiles that might try to eat them.

Survival of the fittest

The bigger they grow, the more independent the young crocodiles get. At first they eat crickets, slugs, and grubs. Then they turn to small birds and rodents. Eventually they hunt big mammals who come near the water to drink.

The young crocodiles keep growing even after they become adults at about ten years old. The bigger they are, the easier it will be to claim territory of their own. Some search downriver while others may try to find a small lake. Wherever they go, they clean up the land around them by eating dead or sick animals along the way.

Now that they are adults, the crocodiles fight to find out which of them is strongest. The winner will get to start a family of its own.

Man-eater?

The crocodile has a reputation for being a terrifying creature that hunts and kills people. Although some species will attack humans who enter their territory, for many years it was humans who hunted the crocodile for its skin and meat. Even today there is a big demand for crocodile parts. Although many crocodiles are now raised on farms, some species are close to extinction.

All of these objects are made from crocodile skins and help push the crocodile closer to extinction.

Fascinating creatures

The crocodile's ancestors appeared on earth over two hundred million years ago. The smallest measured about sixteen inches, and the biggest grew up to fifty feet long. At least one crocodile species lived on every continent.

People have always been fascinated by the crocodile. Prehistoric people painted pictures of crocodiles on cave walls. The ancient Egyptians worshipped a crocodile god named Sobek. In India, the goddess of the sacred river Ganges had a crocodile as a friend. Many African cultures have stories about men who turned into crocodiles.

Some people do not like ranches because they encourage poachers to kill wild crocodiles in order to steal their eggs or young. Ranches and farms also help maintain the crocodile skin market even though they cannot meet all of the demand.

Cultivating crocodiles

To help meet the demand for skins and other crocodile parts, people began farming crocodiles. There are two ways to do it: On ranches, young crocodiles and eggs are taken from the wild; on farms, adult crocodiles are caught and encouraged to have babies who are then fed and protected as they grow up.

Destroyed for their skins

In the eighteenth and nineteenth centuries, rewards were often offered for killing crocodiles. During the twentieth century, crocodile skin became valuable for stylish bracelets, shoes, and purses. Between 1950 and 1980, about three million Nile crocodiles were killed for their skins. Scientists are now trying to protect many crocodile species.

A herpetologist, a scientist who studies reptiles and amphibians, measures eggs to help find out how to protect the crocodile from extinction.

Cousins from around the world

The crocodile is part of a group of animals called crocodilians. In all, there are twenty-three different species in three subfamilies: crocodiles, alligators and caimans, and gharials. The main visible difference among them is the shape of their snouts. In general, the gharial's snout is the narrowest, and the alligator and caiman's is the widest. The alligator's head is also blunter and heavier than the caiman's.

▲ Johnston's crocodile lives in the freshwater lakes and swamps of Australia. Its long, narrow nose helps it to catch fish. Measuring about eight feet long, Johnston's crocodile is one of the smaller crocodile species.

◄ The saltwater crocodile is the biggest member of the family. It can grow up to twenty feet long. The saltwater crocodile lives in oceans, lakes, and large rivers all over the Pacific and tropical Asia.

▲ The jacare is a kind of spectacled caiman. This species gets its name from the bony ridge that makes a bump over each eye. All caimans live only in South America.

▲ The Ganges gharial is the only true gharial alive today. It lives on the Indian subcontinent in deep, quickly flowing rivers. The Ganges gharial uses its long, pincerlike nose to catch frogs and fish.

▲ The American alligator lives only in the southern United States. It is often hunted for the skin on its stomach, which makes soft, strong leather. The American alligator is a protected species in Florida and can often be found near people's homes. This makes some people nervous, but the American alligator rarely attacks humans.

For Further Reading on Crocodilians. . .

Arnosky, Jim. <u>All About Alligators</u>. Scholastic, 1994.

Fowler, Alan. <u>Gator or Croc?</u> Rookie Read-About Science Series. Children's Press, 1996.

Harris, Susan. <u>Crocodiles and Alligators.</u> Franklin Watts, 1980.

Lauber, Patricia. <u>Alligators: A Success Story.</u> Henry Holt, 1994.

To See Crocodilians in Captivity. . .

Folzenlogen, Darcy and Robert. <u>The Guide to American Zoos and Aquariums</u>. Willow Press, 1993.

Many zoos and aquariums also have web sites on the internet. To learn more about their exhibits, go to the following pages on the Yahoo! WWW site:

> **http://dir.yahoo.com/Science/Biology/Zoology/Zoos**
> **http://dir.yahoo.com/Science/Biology/Zoology/Zoos/Aquariums**

Use the Internet to Find Out More about Crocodilians and Other Reptiles. . . .

Animal Bytes: Nile Crocodile. Sea World/ Busch Gardens Tampa Bay.
—Fun facts about conservation, habitat, diet, physical traits, and more!
http://www.seaworld.org/animal_bytes/crocodileab.html

Crocodilians: Natural History and Conservation.
—Crocodilian communication, a biology database, and information about captive care.
http://www.crocodilian.com

Crocodiles, Alligators, and More on the Internet!
—Great bibliographies and several links to informative crocodilian sites.
http://itech.fgcu.edu/faculty/mmeers/bcb/croclinks.html

Nile Crocodile. Defenders of Wildlife.
—Photographs and detailed physical description, plus habitat, range, behavior, and more.
http://198.240.72.81/defenders/nilea.html

See Updated Animal Close-Ups Internet Resources. . . .
> **http://www.charlesbridge.com**

Photograph Credits:

Bios Agency:
J.J. Alcalay: p. 3; A. Fatras: p. 4 (top); M. and C. Denis-Huot: pp. 5 (bottom), 8 (bottom left), 10 (bottom), 14 (top), 20-21 (bottom), 26 (top); Robert/ Bergerot: pp. 4-5; J.L. Klein/ M.L. Hubert: pp. 6 (top), 26 (bottom), 27 (top right); J.L. and F. Ziegler: p. 7; C. Thouvenin: pp. 6 (bottom), 12-13; R. Seitre: pp. 8-9, 8 (bottom right); R. La Harpe: pp. 10 (top), 15, 18-19; D. Heuclin: p. 11; WWF/ M. Harvey: pp. 12 (left), 22-23; P. Vaucoulon: p. 13 (right); M. Laboureur: pp. 12 (right), 21 (top); Nigel Dennis/ Fotonatura: p. 16 (middle); N. Viloteau: pp. 16-17, 25 (bottom); S. Montanari/ Panda Photo: p. 20; Dani/ Jeske: p. 27 (top left); Y. Lefevre: p. 27 (bottom); F. Vidal: p. 24; T. Montfort: p. 25 (top).

Pho.n.e Agency:
J.P. Ferrero/ J.M. Labat: p. 9 (bottom); R. Valter: pp. 14 (bottom), 16 (top and bottom).

With sincere thanks to Roger Bour of France's National Museum of Natural History Reptile and Amphibian Laboratory for his scientific advice.